Roderick Buchanan

Players

Dundee Contemporary Arts

Chasing 1,000 1994

Introduction

This publication and the exhibition it accompanies offer the first oppor-
tunity for the work of Roderick Buchanan to be explored in depth.
Buchanan has become best known recently for his works with video,
works in which he uses the medium in its simplest form, making straight,
real-time recordings or in some instances using found footage from TV
coverage. His use of technology, whether in moving or still imagery, is
transparent: we instantly see through it to the people and places depicted.
It allows immediate access to an awareness of our subjective responses to
and interpretations of appearance. Both photographic and video works
can therefore be seen as contemporary versions of the most traditional of
genres: portraiture and landscape, explorations of the ways in which we
go about investing character in people and places.

His work excavates the territory between the general, universal appearance of what we refer to as global culture and the persistent manifestation
of the local, the individual and the particular. Made with people and on
the street, he looks at how we look, how we appear to each other and how
we go about presenting ourselves to the world.

Formal sports and informal games feature regularly in Buchanan's
practice, examined as a means of assessing how our recreational activities
– what we do with time that is our own – express and communicate identity. Showing us invented children's pastimes on an equal footing with the
Tour de France or the World Cup, Buchanan's interest is not in the competition *per se*, but in the big issues of race, nationality, culture, identity,
aspiration and allegiance which surround the fields of play.

Bishopbriggs 1998

6

Dundee Contemporary Arts is delighted to be bringing this outstanding body of work together for the first time and particularly to include a newly commissioned piece, filmed in Dundee. *Out* is Buchanan's first work to be made in film and furthers his interest in informal street games, familiar from *Sodastream* and *Gobstopper*. The work has been realised with the assistance of many, but we are particularly grateful to Mike Stubbs, Carol Salter and Shaun McBeath for their co-operation.

The works presented in the exhibition have been realised over several years with the support and assistance of many individuals. It is a testament to Buchanan's drive and enthusiasm the extent to which so many have participated in his practice over that time. We are, of course, thankful to all those who have helped in bringing together this exhibition and publication. Particular thanks go to Susanna Beaumont, Mika Hannula, Daniel Jewesbury and Ross Sinclair whose texts contribute to making this publication the first extensive document of Buchanan's diverse and engaging practice. As with any project of this scale, however, the most important contributor has been the artist himself. Buchanan's absolute commitment to the new film, the exhibition and this publication has been outstanding and we are enormously grateful to him for the energy, attention and humour he has brought to their realisation.

Katrina M. Brown *Curator*

Andrew Nairne *Director*

Gobstopper 1999

BUTTER KNIFE

CHEESE KNIFE

DESSERT KNIFE

DINNER KNIFE

FISH KNIFE

STEAK KNIFE

GRAPEFRUIT KNIFE

OYSTER KNIFE

PARING KNIFE

BREAD KNIFE

FILLETING KNIFE

BONING KNIFE

HAM KNIFE

CARVING KNIFE

COOKS KNIFE

CLEAVER

MACHETE

COMMANDO KNIFE

PONIARD

STILETTO

DAGGER

ONE-HANDED SWORD

ONE-AND-A-HALF SWORD

RAPIER

SABRE

TWO-HANDED SWORD

Politics, loyalty and the class of '84

Ross Sinclair

We've known Roddy for more than fifteen years. We've watched his work
emerge over those years. We were in the same year at art school, same
department, Environmental Art, same space, same flats, same friends –
same neighbourhood. We have shown often together, in Scotland, England, Europe, America, Australia and other places too. It's part and parcel
of the whole world we came out of, showing together, dialogue, argument.
We learned a lot from each other – taught each other. We learned a lot
from Roddy.* Back in the day, our work was similar, coming from the same
place. In some ways it still is, although you wouldn't think it at first glance.
But back then everything was open, nothing was fixed, anything was pos-
sible. At that time, when we were students, Glasgow was a hotbed of Neo-
Expressionism. It seemed as though this work had fallen in from another
century. Above all, it was anathema to our need to talk, our desire for dialogue, with each other, with the audience, with anyone who would listen.
Nevertheless, at least it proved to us there was life beyond the backwater.
What was there to lose by looking to the wider world? We were the *avant-
garde*, the new breed, and now we are the mainstream.

* I remember once seeing him adding some
text to a piece of work which was in a
horrible typeface. I asked him why he was
using this no frills basic typeface when
another would surely make the work look
better. He explained to me that it wasn't
supposed to make the piece 'look good'
but was supposed to make it work.

List of Blades 1993

**Roddy Buchanan
and Ross Sinclair**
Galerie Knoll,
Vienna, 1993

10   The infectious self-determination of those days has produced a genera-
tion of Scottish artists who are quite simply the best there has ever been.
Roddy has always been at the heart of it – the planning, the scheming, the
discussions, the arguments, the passion, the integrity, the location of the
core of identity. National and international, horizontally developing infra-
structures – Glasgow to Amsterdam, Glasgow to Berlin, Glasgow to Paris,
Glasgow to New York, L.A. wherever and all on return tickets – fuck
London, we thought, who needs it? (though we always kept in touch).
Throughout these years of argument, debate and discussion Roddy has
always demonstrated an innate talent for controversy. I can't quite think
how else to put it. He makes things happen. He is passionate. Sometimes
he is reckless and insensitive, provocative and aggressive. Sometimes he
goes too far. But his work is perceptive and precise, and it travels its own
path. It works on the same premise as his personality. He knows who you
are. He knows where you live. Metaphorically speaking of course. Roddy
knows us well, even after all these years, and sometimes it can be disturb-
ing. We both came from the suburbs, not cred, not cool, just blank. But the
thing about Roddy is that in the last 15 years he hasn't lost a desire, a need
to push things as far as they can go, to cut through the polite conversation
of cosmopolitan art and the aspirational lifestyle of its practitioners. In his
work, and sometimes in his life. Of course some people don't like it.

    Loyalty is very important. It cuts through Roddy's work from the very
beginning. Loyalty to background, your school, your class, your country,

Mid-Atlantic Tartan
1986

your team, your mates, the crown, your gang, your ideals. Not just your own idea of loyalty, of course, but how this concept changes in different cultures, different places, different times.

So here's a salutory tale about loyalty. It has etched itself into the core of our relationship. I think most people he knows well have a story like this. It happened to us sometime in the late eighties. I don't exactly remember when. We were rolling home to the flat we shared, in the early hours of the morning after a Ramones gig, both absolutely drunk. The road we were walking took us through a park that the police patrolled regularly. Sure enough, a police van crawled by and I made the mistake of gesticulating rather too enthusiastically in its general direction. It pulled over and we were collared. Unless you've been asked, you can't imagine how ridiculous 'What's your name, sonny', sounds at 3am on a dark Glasgow street. While I dutifully answered in my best slurred suburbs accent Roddy answered sharply, 'Roger Ramjet'. Five minutes later he was handcuffed in the back of the van and the cop turned to me and asked if I wanted to join my smartarse friend in the back of the van. I replied simply, 'no'. 'Well fuck off home then', I was strongly advised. Rightly or wrongly Roddy never forgave me. That breach of loyalty was anathema to him. I supposed he couldn't understand it, it was us against them, wasn't it? The moment passed, but it has been the source of an unresolved barrier between us ever since. Together we were strong, but I let them divide and conquer. Of course, I now wish I'd gone with him. Because nothing really came of it. So

Warning: MORE THA

I imagine us, brothers in arms in the back of the black Mariah, standing together against the forces of oppression, then telling the story for years to come as our friends cried, 'not again'. Sadly the fact is, if it happened again tomorrow I'd probably do the same thing.

Roddy's early work around this time was politically informed, politically motivated. Printed tartans with Polaris submarines in fashion shows, plaster petrol bombs, milk churn bombs, flags, graffiti (official and unofficial). Formally diverse and rich, intellectually striving, politics and struggle elevated by a curious mix of clean edges and revolutionary colour schemes. He worked for a whole year on a series of billboard interventions during a year out from art school. He wanted do this outside of the restrictions of the academic process. We lived together at that time and I would regularly hear him going out in the middle of the night, sometimes several times in one night, to make his billboard works. These were generally based on the space at the bottom of the poster filled with government health warnings on tobacco advertisements. First he would paint out the warnings, then would return a few hours later when it was dry to complete the *détournement*, often proposing a new relationship between this new text and the existing image, sometimes unaltered, sometimes radically changed. No graffiti scrawl this, no polarised politics. The attention to detail was immense.

These works were sophisticated and beautiful, politically charged and aesthetically sublime. But he still had to dodge the cops. Often these

works were very subtle, the antithesis of a more overtly politicised political graffiti popular at the time. In many ways this was their great strength. The uncertainty and confusion provoked by these new images provided a more powerful and unsettling experience for the viewer, if they happened to notice something was different. His work has always challenged the viewer in this way, and has sought a more profound relationship with a small number of viewers rather that a catch all, something for everyone strategy. Sometimes his works do not readily announce themselves as ART, and consequently possess a great power and possibility for real engagement. Nevertheless these works needed the public, they relied on a context, and they were slow burners, though often they didn't last long. I'm sure there are some he never even managed to photograph.

In one of his works from *Guilt by Association*, 1992, he spent the months before the show documenting the meetings between the artists and their meetings with Declan McGonagle (illustrated above). This work captured the dynamics of these long discussions about the nature of the show, and this particular group of artists. He was striving to document the process of this collaboration. And to show these in the Irish Museum of Modern Art in Dublin served to emphasise the assertion that this debate, this process, these questions – How can we make an exhibition? How can it be coherent? How can our individual concerns come together to make something which is more that the sum of the parts? – were just as important as what was on the walls at the end.

Outing Art
BBC billboard commission
1992

Social Security
1990

To nobody's surprise, in 1989 he went to study for an MA in Belfast, with Alastair MacLennan. The draw of the city was overwhelming for Roddy. The conflict, the contradictions, the abuse of power, the history and the geography. His investigation of the relationship between politics and aesthetics continued apace over his year there. Roddy is a great explorer of people and places, whether it's wandering up to the Bronx on his skateboard on a student trip to New York and nearly missing the plane home, or his late night walks around Belfast, through all the places you shouldn't really go. I accompanied him on one of these trips and while we walked cautiously various routes through the places well-known from news footage and a hundred songs, discussing the complexities of this complicated city and its war, he was at great pains to avoid any inference of cultural or political tourism. He was living there and expressed the utmost respect for the complexities of history. But still, he wanted to see for himself.

There is another important aspect of Roddy's practice and it's a kind of work ethic that flows through its various forms. From the earliest works there has been something of a process of production evident. This is certainly clear in the intensive dedication of the year long billboard series, or the casting of hundreds of plaster relief crowns attached permanently to temporary walls at his MA show in the foyer of the art school at the University of Ulster in Belfast and in *Self Conscious State*, 1990, at Third Eye Centre in Glasgow. There was the project on a bus shelter in Glasgow where he made silk screen prints on coloured sheets of paper which each

figured a single head, copied from the masthead of *The Guardian*. These
were then attached to each panel of the bus shelter and changed every day.
The installation looked like a continually evolving flag of a non-nation
with mysterious, statesman-like figures at the centre of each colour.
People would come to the shelter every day, waiting around for their bus.
This captive audience would witness this strange transformation and try
to piece together the fractured narrative. Then there's *Ten in a Million* ...
I remember helping him make one version in Amsterdam and I can vouch
for the difficulty in organising this not to mention the uncomfortable
practicalities of producing it. It's a sign of his passion for the project that
he has made this work in nine cities now. However, this allows him to ex-
plore these cities where this series has been made, an excuse, if one were
needed, to go native. This process continues in the *Coast to Coast, Dennistoun* series. This project has spread over four years and has necessitated
Roddy going out, countless times, on the streets of Glasgow's east end,
approaching gangs of teenagers, asking to photograph them and their
baseball caps. In one sense the images from these projects are merely the
record of the process of investigation, the journey. This is significant in
many of his works. There also seems to be a desire in this process to put
himself in uncomfortable or challenging circumstances while making the
work. Making himself vulnerable.

    We have all changed quite a lot in the past decade. There is no longer
the same proximity between us. This little group has exploded out into the

the same proximity between us. This little group has exploded out into the world. Everyone is on their own trajectory and it's now common to go for months or sadly, years, without seeing the new work of someone of whom you used to know every nuance of the tiniest thing they did. We all feel that loss, but I think Roddy feels it a little more than most. I know he still feels the first audience for his work is his peer group. While living in New York a few years ago he worked as an art shipper. 3000 miles away from home, schlepping Monets and Rymans in and out of Upper West Side apartments. I remember seeing a photo of him, I don't remember whether it was a work or just a snap. He was standing by a big truck on a New York street wearing a white T-shirt with black text clearly visible on the front. It read simply, 'Be true to your school'.

Friends vs. Other Friends

Susanna Beaumont

According to the writer J. G. Ballard, a car travelling along an unknown road to an unknown destination is the image that most succinctly sums up modern life. Roderick Buchanan, like the rest of us, has inhabited such an image. As a keen young footballer, Buchanan and his football mates were frequently driven along unknown roads to unknown pitches in his native Glasgow by football dads. From the backseat of a Bedford van or a Ford family saloon, through steamed-up windows and an air heavy with teenage bravado, Glasgow unfurled before him at a steady 30mph. He deciphered seams between suburbs and registered the street activity of a neighbourhood. At traffic lights or in tailbacks, the urban terrain was momentarily freeze-framed. Buchanan mapped out a city clustered around arterial roads and residential side streets.

These journeys, made in the name of away-day football fixtures, transported Buchanan just a matter of miles. But mileage enough to make him a member of a visiting side, out to play the opposition on their home ground. It set in motion a fascination with home and away, teams and identity, cultural exchange and geographical movement. Today Buchanan frequently exhibits abroad. Lengthy visits to a global spread of cities and towns have replaced away-day fixtures in a single metropolis. Buchanan annually travels thousands of air miles at an average cruising speed of 500mph. At an altitude of 36,000ft, you are hard pressed to decipher the seams between continents, let alone the cultural climate of the land mass below.

In his short essay, 'Mobile Notes', Buchanan listed the destinations he

Coast to Coast,
Dennistoun (detail)
1996–2000

Bondi Beach, Sydney September 2000

travelled to in 1996. Paris – Liverpool – Nîmes – Paris – Berlin – Stockholm – Manchester – Amsterdam – Paris – Glasgow – Rheims – New York ran the itinerary. 'How', he asks, 'do you make sense of that lot?' He's in good company. In his novel *Invisible Cities*, Italo Calvino imagines a dialogue between the 13th century traveller Marco Polo and the Emperor Kublai Khan. The emperor notes that 'you recognise cities better on the atlas than when you visit them in person'. Marco Polo replies, 'Travelling you realise that differences are lost: each city takes to resembling all cities … Your atlas preserves the differences intact: the assortment of qualities which are like letters in a name'. Over seven centuries on, Buchanan is a frequent-flyer inhabitant of the global village, investigating cultural divides, national boundaries and inter-city relations.

We humans have a propensity for ordering. In attempting to tidy up the world, we find common characteristics to attach to diversity. We talk of the developed world and the developing world; the West and the East; the United Kingdom and mainland Europe; urban and rural. In seizing on polarities, we make maps in our minds, to enable us to position ourselves in the world. We define ourselves in relation to the other. For Marco Polo a range of destinations was ordered into a near-indistinguishable collection of foreign cities. Differences camouflaged by common characteristics. For Buchanan, an international itinerary throws up an intriguing confusion. Glasgow looks very different to New York on paper but what are the differences on the ground? In Glasgow, Buchanan is at home, in New York he is away. In short, each city has different associations for him. A city's

Players who associate themselves with Italian football by wearing Inter Milan and A.C. Milan shirts amid the dozens of local tops on display every night on the football parks of Glasgow.

identity does not simply lie in its 'look' but in the memory, assumptions and prejudices that come to mind when we think about it.

Buchanan's work gently interrogates the idea that identity lies in the eye and the mind of the beholder. How, when confronted with the unfamiliar, we frequently seek out something with which we can identify. In excavating issues of identity and association, Buchanan frequently uses the medium of sport. It is familiar territory for him, who declares that he still feels at home on a football pitch. Football like many other sports, is dependent on the concept of opposing teams. Membership of a particular team is signposted by a uniform, which in turn aids our ability to identify with one team.

Work in Progress, 1995, consists of a series of portrait photographs of footballers. The players have the familiar pose of the football fanzine pin-up: arms at their sides looking directly at the camera. They wear football shirts of the rival Italian clubs A.C. Milan and Inter Milan. We assume they are the Italian players. But these men are no Euro professionals. Players plucked from amateur five-a-side teams, they are Glasgow men who have appropriated the uniform of Milanese football teams, symbolic of something to which they adhere or aspire. Milanese shirts are symbolic of style, success, even masculine prowess. In the mid 1990s, Italian teams were widely venerated for their on-pitch skills and valour and by buying into their look, these Glasgow amateurs have adopted a succinct allusion to a complex web of characteristics. They have joined the team. Milanese style can of course go out of fashion, and another look must then be

Endless Column 1999

26

adopted to indicate another set of aspirations or membership to another team. But *Work In Progress* is disconcerting. It is not simply a record of Glasgow footballers but rather an exposé of how we can be misled by uniform. On first reading, we believe the players to be something that they are not. Buchanan has exposed the perils of judging by appearances.

In the video work, *Endless Column*, 1999, Buchanan further teases out our habitual and deeply subjective interpretation of appearances. A camera runs along teams of rugby players standing in line prior to kick off. It records the moment when national anthems are played, when players evoke either a godhead or plain good luck to propel them to victory. Edited to produce a ceaseless, silent column of men, as one face leads to another face, so one team blends into another. It is an extended, multi-national identity parade. As a viewer, you find yourself somewhat uneasily, even guiltily, attempting to discern a 'national type' to indicate which team you might be looking at. But in uniting the teams, Buchanan has taken away our bearings, uprooted the reference points of nationhood. Our allegiances have nowhere to go, our means of identification removed. In *Turnaround*, 1998 allegiances are again confounded. Identical footage of the 1998 England v Italy football match is screened simultaneously on two video monitors. From one monitor we hear the Italian commentary, from the other the English commentary, each accompanied by a translation in subtitles. We are given two interpretations of the same match. 'Tribal loyalties' are toyed with and national stereotypes are at play. Seeing the game from the Italian point of view, the arbitrariness of allegiances is made ap-

raggruppamenti, altre sette. Una grande occasione qui, stasera, per l'Inghilterra, ma non sottovalutate

Ball towards Zola, who is marked by the defender Batty and passed to Campbell.

parent. The Italian side is good, they play well and the commentary seems fair. The other side has become less 'other'. Moreover the Italian team do not demonstrate the supposedly characteristic, hot-blooded Mediterranean temperament any more than the fast-talking English commentary is exemplary of the supposedly English trait of stiff-upper lip reserve.

In 1995 when in the Welsh town of Llandudno, Buchanan asked his companion if the local inhabitants looked Welsh. Back at home, Buchanan asked 'if there was a Glaswegian look?' In mainland Europe war had broken out in the Balkans and the phrase 'ethnic cleansing' made its debut in the English language. With *Work in Progress* and *Endless Column*, Buchanan has subverted the signposts that direct the way we see a nation and a national type. We don't know where we stand.

'Sport is a valuable tool politically and socially. It is a boom industry' believes Buchanan. And it is an industry with a history. Sports events are familiar players in political power games. In 1936, Hitler notoriously attempted to use the Berlin Olympics as a means to prove the superiority of the Aryan race. Sport, like politics, can get in to the wrong hands. And today with the advent of satellite television and global media networks sport has never been so powerful. 'Media rights' revenue has become the driving force behind all sport' according to Jean-Paul de la Fuente, chief executive of the sports media consultants, Media Content. So it's hardly surprising that *The Guardian* newspaper's 2000 list of the fifty most influential people in sport puts Rupert Murdoch at number one. Murdoch is the famously non-sport playing man behind Sky, Fox and Star TV networks. It makes perfect sense that the recent Sydney Olympics were used as a platform to announce to the world Australia's improved inter-race relations, with the Aboriginal athlete, Cathy Freeman, lighting the Olympic torch.

But does sport have a role to play in what has been described as 'new internationalism', where global order is supposedly becoming less concerned with geographical boundaries? 'Borders are just the scars of history ... in this current age of globalisation, nation states have become so last century' proclaims the hi-gloss life and style magazine, *Wallpaper** in an article titled 'New World'. Regionalism and the border-less city-state are the future. Yet exclusion zones remain, based if not on geography then on your financial reserves. Checking in to the New World costs money.

One of surest ways of checking in to the New World is to adopt its national dress. If sport is now a global industry, sportswear is now a globally-accessible uniform. Sportswear has evolved into leisurewear into everyday streetwear. It has colonised high streets throughout the world. To wear trainers does not require training. Armchair supporters and non-spectators can be fully paid-up members of a global sporting empire. Somewhat ironic, as we play at looking sporty in an age when members of the Western world are showing increased couch potato tendencies. But for Buchanan, every piece of sportswear tells a story about fantasies and alliances. Buchanan, like an anthropologist, frequently takes to the streets, to gauge the currents in sportswear, or rather to gauge the subtle but significant shifts in chosen allegiances.

In the 1970s, a discreet Fred Perry logo could often be spied on pastel-coloured sports shirts favoured by men fond of golf on a Sunday. An avant-garde 'logo' soldier, it arguably marked the liberation of the label/logo from the inside shirt collar to its confident take-over of the shirtfront and sleeve. In the 1980s, young men with sharp haircuts who wanted to cut a sartorial dash on urban thoroughfares rather than the golf course, appropriated Fred Perry shirts with their familiar laurel logo. Same uniform but a very different team. This interests Buchanan. In *Yankees*, 1997, Buchanan photographed anyone he came across on his travels wearing the NY insignia of the New York baseball team, the Yankees. The resulting line-up was a motley crew of individuals spotted across Continental Europe united by an insignia.

In *Coast to Coast, Dennistoun*, 1996–2000, Buchanan photographed individuals sporting an article of clothing emblazoned with a North American sports club logo. This time his catchment area was limited to the Glasgow neighbourhood of Dennistoun. In this 'whitebread' community, lads wear elaborately sloganed caps and sweatshirts of a far distant country's sporting teams. But Buchanan is not playing the tourist in other people's reality or fashion statements. It is more that he is trying to tease out why a Glasgow boy chooses a North American game cap and a Turkish immigrant in Berlin wears a Yankees baseball cap. Arguably an ever-changing geo-political landscape coupled with effective marketing tactics has strengthened the appeal of signing-up for an 'invincible' American sports team. Yet on the streets of Berlin or Glasgow, another set of alle-

Coast to Coast, Dennistoun
Installation view, West Scaland
Museum of Art, Soro, 1998

giances is doubtless at work. The wearers of club-branded clothes attach their own personalised meaning to what they wear and what they see others wear. Local teams and alliances are not wholly drowned out by allegiances to international sports teams.

Spectators at the Olympics were asked to declare if they were in possession of knives, weapons or cans of Pepsi. The said drink was then confiscated to prevent upsetting the fizzy drink monopoly of a principal sponsor, Coca-Cola. It is not with little effort that Coca-Cola is reportedly the world's second most recognised word after OK. Or so their PR machine tells us. Buchanan, however, has an eye on more local drink manufacturers.

Sodastream, 1995, pays homage to the Glasgow-made soft drink's company, Garvies, who count bitter lemon crush, super bitter lemon crush and lemon crush among their nineteen flavours of fizzy pop. Coca-Cola may be out to quench the globe's thirst but Garvies can offer the thirsty a different flavour daily for a fortnight. In this video work, a succession of hand-held bottles of candy-coloured pop are dropped on to a concrete floor. The bottles smash and the liquid breaks out to form fizzing puddles. As bottles repeatedly fall, the contents mingle on the concrete floor, and are homogenised into a swirling mass. The complete range of nineteen bottles is reduced to smithereens. In *Sodastream*, Buchanan delivers a message in broken bottles, but it is also a celebration of childhood pleasure. *Gobstopper*, 1999, likewise relishes childhood delight. A fourteen minute video projection, it records a succession of young children attempting to

Sodastream
1995,
video stills

Gobstopper 1999

hold their breath as they are driven in a camper van through Glasgow's Clyde Tunnel. It is a long tunnel. It takes fifty seconds for the van to travel from one side to the other but the children, with varying degrees of delight and rivalry, hold tight their breath with alarming success. Watching the video, eavesdropping on the private world of these children, you are inevitably tempted to join in, to try it, to flirt with the small-time but real danger of not breathing. It is a challenge and you marvel at their ability to hold their breath. The engaged spectator is left breathless.

Buchanan's on-going interest in the ways that individuals create their own private worlds in public places is perhaps most evocatively explored in *Out*, 2000, his new film commissioned by Dundee Contemporary Arts. In it, Buchanan focuses on a lone skater spiralling down a car park ramp. It is an anonymous space. It could be in any one of the countless concrete high-rise car parks that punctuate the urbanscape of the Western world. It is also a sort of no-man's land. Car drivers park and don't linger, walking briskly on. Yet these monuments to the age of the car, provide a venue for skating, an informal and individual pursuit. It seems an illicit activity, to appropriate a building built for practical purposes for private pleasure.

If J. G. Ballard believes a moving car is a symbol of the modern age, it follows that the high-rise car park is its indispensable accessory. Buchanan's work is rooted in this modern age. Walk into a pub and there's live sport beamed in from a far-off country courtesy of Sky TV. At half-time come ads for Nike trainers and a news bulletin on the resurgence of ethnic unrest in the Balkans. Back out on the street some guy is wearing a

Yankee baseball cap and not far away the local five-a-side football team are kicking a ball around a pitch wearing a pick'n mix selection of international football shirts. On the side-lines a young kid is shaking a bottle of Coca-Cola to improve the fizz and a middle-aged woman ambles past in jogging pants.

Buchanan alerts us to this everyday landscape of life at home and away. What do we make of it? It is the meeting point, the seemingly seamless integration of global politics through to mass-marketed merchandise into the local landscape that Buchanan intelligently investigates. How we define our identity by identifying with or against others. It is sensitive territory but Buchanan is not an indifferent spectator on the lives of others. He wears a Raiders sweatshirt, plays football when he can and speculates about the Premier League. Buchanan's skill is to throw up engaging questions about the world we live in.

Deadweight 2000
Installation view, Museum of
Contemporary Art, Sydney

Deadweight

Outboxed in the opener, Mike Tyson's crouch-ing attacks were being countered by a series of right uppercuts in the second. By the 4th his left eye had started to swell and the injury progressively worsened until he was peering through a slit. Finding it difficult to get inside those long jabs and whipping uppercuts, he knew he was being steadily out-pointed. Dropping behind, Tyson found a perfect right uppercut to floor his opponent in the 8th. It had been his last chance. In the 9th he took a merciless pounding and in the 10th a right uppercut and a four-punch combination sent him to the canvas.

Deadweight

Holding the WBC title, Esteban de Jesus brought his lightweight championship belt to this unifica-tion bout. With 21 rounds of experience between the fighters it was never going to be the explo-sive affair of previous encounters. Patiently outboxed, he managed to keep himself in the fight until the 12th round. However, 2 minutes, 32 seconds into that round, he met the punch that knocked him out and ended his hopes of uniting the titles.

'It is so important that a German won. And even more so that it was a runner with white legs.' Petra Schumann, mother of the 800 metre Olympic winner in Sydney, Nils Schumann

Tulla Puun Takaa Coming from Behind the Tree

Mika Hannula

It is no secret that to get some substance into any story, it is the local rather than the global on which you need to focus. You must try to be particular, specific and contextual. You must simply tell your version of the story, a story whose significance stems from the little local details and nuances that make things matter. The other part of the deal, which often tends to be forgotten, is that you also need someone to listen.

Change Up
1998, video
installation

What follows is my version of a story. A story in three parts, recounting the three most important ice hockey games of the past few decades. (A small hint: what football might be to Scots, ice hockey is for Finns.) My proposition is that this story allows not only a comparison between two nations who have always loved to be the very second best, but also offers no less than a condensed view of the post-war history of a tiny nation state called Finland.

The first match takes us back to 1974 – the time of Finlandization, when we lived in the shadow of the Soviet Union. The world championships are in Helsinki. It is the last game of the tournament, and the Finns beat the Czechs, winning the bronze medal, their first ever in international competition. I was watching the game with my grandfather on his black and white TV set. We were both very happy, going out for a stroll after the game, walking on a bitterly cold winter afternoon on the ice in front of their cottage on the south coast of Finland. The celebrations lasted for 4 hours. After that, there was a news flash on the radio. The hero of the game, the Finnish goalie, had tested positive for high levels of ephedrine. This meant trouble. Due to the doping, the jury disqualified the Finns. The result: Finland dropped out of the medals. The result for the family: I remember helping my grandfather prepare the sauna, him standing on the ice, looking sadly to the flat frozen horizon. I saw him crying. He came into the sauna to help me out, wiping his eyes and complaining how the strong wind outside had brought tears to his eyes.

The second game takes us to Moscow, year 1986. Again, it's the world championships. A story best told by Janne, a very close friend of mine (in fact my defense partner in our hockey team for many years) who experienced it at first hand. It was Finland's final game, this time against Sweden. The third period, 50 seconds left. 50 seconds until they could at last claim their first medal. Janne was in Moscow taking part in a youth hockey tournament and watched the game with an American player named Brett Hull, son of the famous Bobby Hull, record-breaking NHL player; Brett went on to break some of the scoring records of his father).

Finland were leading 4–2, with a face-off in the centre. It looked so good. Then something really horrible happened. A Finnish defender got the puck and instead of simply sending the puck into the neutral zone, he tried to do something fancy. He failed miserably. The Swedish player Mats Sundin (also to become one of the best players in NHL) got a free shot and scored

There were still 35 seconds to go. And then it happened again, exactly as before. The Finnish coach didn't even bother to change the line up – and yes, there were still 15 seconds left to play and the game was 4–4. Again, it meant no medals for Finland. Understandably, my friend was furious. By that time, most of the Finns, and particularly Mr. Hull, were also extremely full of cheap vodka. The result: violence and aggression, chairs broken and bottles thrown on to the ice, and at some point the riot police were sent in, my friend and his American acquaintance ending up in a police strangle-hold. However, after being booked, Mr. Hull paid them both off, giving $100 to the main officer. He also paid for the rest of the night as they went on drinking, my friend weeping, really crying. Crying, I suppose, like only a young man can whose dreams have just been shattered.

Now comes the tricky part. Local stories must be partial, but are they always also patriotic and patriarchal? Are they dangerous, just fun – or slightly pathetic? The well-known saving grace of both the Finns and the Scots is that there are so few of us. After all, in such small numbers we can't be harmful. Our interest in sports is purely a sign of healthy nationalism, isn't it? Just good fun, no racism or bigotry intended. Nothing like the nationalism apparent in the comment made by the mother of the winner of the Olympic 800 meter final?

The last game took place in 1995 in Stockholm. It was the final of the tournament, the classic: Finland against Sweden. Finland were coached for the first time by a Swedish guy, who was able to really motivate the team. Against the odds, I think, Finland won and by a good margin of

5–2. Finland were the world champions. An achievement long overdue. When they returned home, over 100,000 people celebrated with them in the main square of Helsinki. A bigger crowd than any previous gathering in peace time in Finland. And right there, right then, they screamed themselves out of the collective misery of low self-esteem. Finland could at last claim their gold medal.

Change Up 1998
video installation

Peloton

Daniel Jewesbury

We think of sport in terms of allegiance and competition. We witness it as a narrative performed and unfurled on an epic, heroic scale, even when it's compressed into the twenty-one inches of a TV set. As we watch, depending on the extent of our investment, we share our anxiety and elation with the rest of the crowd, or the rest of the bar, or our partners. Even if we are not physically in the stadium we can feel affiliated. It goes the other way too; we fantasise that we feel the emotions of the players themselves; they are, after all, doing it for us.

Roderick Buchanan makes art about sport, as a means of exciting dialogue about our broader social behaviour. In the cultures of various sports, Buchanan shows us endlessly-varied microcosms: the team or the crowd, or the supporters thousands of miles away, as the social unit, and within that unit, the adhesion, affiliation, aggression and fragmentation of everyday life. Buchanan does not separate the sport from the context of its reproduction for the spectator or enthusiast, or the conditions governing that reproduction. He does not deal with sport as a self-contained abstraction but as a set of phenomena engaged in a mutual discourse with the regulations of society, both influential and influenced.

Buchanan's installation *Peloton* is a four-hour videotape, onto which the 1998 Tour de France has been distilled. Buchanan has pared away everything except the aerial views of the main pack (or peloton): gone are the leaders, the sprints and chases, the interviews and ceremonies. There is arguably a narrative to this strange feature film: the '98 Tour began in Ireland and ended, as always, on the Champs Elysée in Paris, and one

Peloton 1999
video still

occasionally recognises something of the landscape, particularly as the piece reaches its anti-climax. More usually, however, the riders move inexorably onward through anonymous surroundings. Surveyed from above like this, the peloton appears to be not many riders but one elastic, rolling, amorphous superorganism. Riders drop off, the pack reforms: the character of the whole is unchanged. The movement of helicopter and camera combines with the perpetual motion of the peloton to produce a mesmeric effect.

In cinema, camera movement is used to reveal to the viewer some piece of information: but here the camera pans, again and again, to nothing new. It is as if this were an exercise in Structuralist film from the 1970s: Buchanan has taken all the crucial elements – protagonists, setting, plot and camera movement – and diverted them, to focus the viewer on just one thing: the movement of the peloton through the landscape. Occasional interruptions (traffic on a flyover, a herd of cattle running alongside the race, the shadow of the helicopter flickering on the treetops) distance us momentarily from the action, but the real 'events', as established in the first few seconds, remain unaffected. At times this relentless suspense can seem comical: where *are* these people going? What is driving them on? Why don't they stop and have a look at the scenery?

As the riders pass a roundabout, or turn through a hairpin bend, the pack swells and stretches. As it flows from the inside to the outside edge of the lane, rounding a bend designed to be taken at seventy miles per hour, the peloton describes the line of least resistance in the roadway in minute

detail. Occasionally, the saturated colours of the team jerseys are like the
iridescent shells of scurrying beetles.

What Roderick Buchanan shows us in this and a number of other works is the relationship between player and spectator, and how affiliation and 'social relationships' are central even to the most commercialised of sports. *Peloton* examines the spectacle of sport and the strange power of the spectator, the exhaustive, unblinking, impossible gaze of the camera-as-spectator, suspended above the ground. Other works invert the positions of player and spectator. In the ongoing series of videos *Ten in a Million*, the camera pans twice through a 360° view of any one of the various municipal football pitches that Buchanan has visited around the world (so far, the series comprises views from Glasgow, Budapest, Amsterdam, Nantes, New York, Manchester, Berlin, Vienna and Trondheim). Located on the centre spot, the camera looks out from the deserted pitch to survey, again and again, the absent crowd. This motif is also used in the video installation *Change Up*, in which the two goals of an ice-hockey pitch are projected at opposite ends of the gallery. The players, all wearing the jerseys of the various teams that they as spectators follow, circle endlessly, exiting from one shot to appear moments later at the other end of the room, behind the opposite goal. The viewer-spectator, standing in the notional area of play, is corralled by the players, who show no interest either in playing or in closing in for the kill.

The unblinking eye of the camera, floating above the frantic, unstoppable peloton, shows to television viewers a scene they could never see

Paramaribo, Suriname

Nantes, France

were they to attend the race itself; the aerial view (whether it is a photo-graph or a map) is compelling because it shows us something that it is not normally within our power to see. It is beguiling, inviting us to believe that we can extend our selves and truly know our surroundings. The extension of 'scopic', or visual, power through the camera results in ever-more definitive surveys of the landscape, ever-more accurate renderings of the world.

Previously, cartography was an approximate business, a sublime blend of leading-edge technology with artistic licence and intelligent guesswork. The irony is that as our maps grow more precise, so they become ever more approximate; able to show previously unrecordable levels of detail, they fix the transient even as it disappears or transforms before our eyes. At a certain point the map ceases to be an iconic representation of space and becomes an object in its own right; the map is utopia, because it is space perfected *and mastered*. Thomas McDonough, quoting Michel de Certeau, writes, 'The elevation provided by the "overflight at high altitude" transforms the sociologist into a voyeur of sorts, who not only enjoys the erotics of seeing all from his hidden vantage point, but who also enjoys the erotics of knowing all ... But this ... is imaginary, a fiction, and the "voyeur-god created by this fiction ... must disentangle himself from the murky in-tertwining daily behaviours and make himself alien to them". *

At first glance, Roderick Buchanan might seem to be enforcing the scopic power of the spectator, the 'voyeur-god'; and yet the space he shows is cut up, fragmented and re-arranged. Sometimes it seems that we are watching the race in real time; some of the cuts between shots seem to suggest continuity of action from one scene to the next. In addition, during the piece's exhibition in Montpellier, the 1999 Tour was actually taking place, watched in bars and cafés all around the town. But the longer we believe in it, the more extreme is our disorientation when we have to 'disentangle' ourselves, when some obvious discontinuity opens up before our eyes. Buchanan constructs a non-place in non-time, as the camera-eye rambles deliriously through abstract space. 'LIVE', says the box in the corner of the projection; in the obsessive 'NOW' that Buchanan has created, the race ceases to be a recording, and becomes maddeningly urgent all over again each time a new viewer starts to watch, to attempt the reconstitution of its broken space.

This re-configuring and distortion of space recalls the work of Stan Douglas, whose impossible panoramas and cyclical narratives also invite the viewer to inhabit a hostile, unknowable space-and-time. But whilst Douglas fabricates ever more elaborate and intricate environments, Buchanan presents us with the base elements – the units – from an unfamiliar perspective. Like Douglas, Buchanan also draws on landscape genres; *Peloton* takes us through these in sequence, sometimes in startling juxtaposition, while *Ten in a Million* displays its peripheral, municipal landscapes on a row of monitors.

In each of the locations, Buchanan has recorded views from ten different football pitches, each time with the same insistently classifying gaze. These views of each city might appear to 'represent' that place, but it

Iona, Scotland

Numeralla, Australia

Ten in a Million (on-going)
Installation view, Glasgow Print Studio

Marseille, France

54   is often the case that we, as viewers, impose our *idea* of that place when we read the title; so 'New York' becomes related to the New York of personal experience or of a million pop icons. The piece is an exercise in comparative landscapes: all of us, when visiting somewhere new, feel the urge to relate it to a place we already know. There is a certain relief that one can find familiarity in a potentially alienating environment; but also there's disappointment that it is not more like itself, whatever we have decided that should be.

Thus, we compare our preconceptions with the places shown, we compare the ten pitches to one another, and we compare the different cities to each other. Since each new view is shown in exactly the same way, it is as if Buchanan is inviting us to make comparisons. Furthermore, the ninety pitches are united by the fact that nearly all of them are on a certain category of land, in residential areas a certain distance from the city centre; the edges of towns that one would never normally see as a tourist. In their presentation and description, the videos set up a 'touristic' logic only to frustrate that approach through their content. Here the piece echoes the structure of *Peloton*, which inveigles the viewer with its compelling visuality, only to confound expectations and force the viewer to re-negotiate. Buchanan, a winger who learnt geography by travelling to play football each week, shows us the whole of the industrialised world in this (ever-expanding) microcosm.

The piece returns again to landscape metaphors with its concentration on 'drawing' in space. The two prerequisites of each of the sites Buchanan

films are that the pitch should have a centre circle marked out, and should
have goal posts. As the camera pans round, the line of the centre circle
becomes a horizontal, bisecting the monitor a third of the way up into two
spaces. This incidental reference to classical rules of composition reminds
us that each of these pitches becomes, when not in use, a kind of drawing,
and moreover, a drawing that is replicated millions of times around the
world. In the more or less haphazardly planned suburbs that Buchanan
shows, the art already exists; it simply requires viewers (players).

Out

Film commissioned by Dundee Contemporary Arts, 2000

Roderick Buchanan
b. 1965 Glasgow

2000 Dundee Contemporary Arts *

Galerie Praz-Delavallade, Paris

1999 FRAC Languedoc Roussillon, Montpellier *

1998 'Turnaround', Hayward Gallery, London *

Galerie Praz-Delavallade, Paris

'Play and Record', Catalyst Arts, Belfast (with Fanni Niemi-Junkola)

1997 Lotta Hammer Gallery, London

YYZ Gallery, Toronto

1996 Jack Tilton Gallery, New York (with Jacqueline Donachie) *illustrated above*

Mai de la Photo, Reims *

1995 City Racing, London (with David Allen)

Glasgow Print Studio

'Work in Progress', Project Room, Tramway, Glasgow *

1994 Knoll Galeria, Budapest (with Ross Sinclair)

1993 Galerie Knoll, Vienna (with Ross Sinclair)

* *denotes a publication accompanied the exhibition*

selected group exhibitions

2000 'Au-delà du spectacle', Centre Georges Pompidou, Paris

'Face On', Site Gallery, Sheffield *

'Sporting Life', Museum of Contemporary Art, Sydney *

'La Beauté de geste', Centre d'Art Contemporain Vassivière-en-Limousin *

'Transfert', Art dans l'espace urbain, Biel-Bienne *

Printemps de Cahors *

Salon de Montrouge, Paris *

'Game On', Sara Meltzer Gallery, New York *

'If I Ruled the World' (part 2), CCA, Glasgow *

'Beck's Futures' ICA, London; Cornerhouse, Manchester; CCA, Glasgow *

'In Consistency', Arthouse, Dublin

'Radio Tuesday', Helsinki

'Become Like Me', Stills Gallery, Edinburgh; An Tuireann, Skye *illustrated above: Endless Column*

'Let's Entertain', Walker Arts Center, Minneapolis *

'Black Box Recorder', British Council Touring Exhibition

'Shoot', Kunsthalle, Malmö *

1998 'Multiples x 1', Temple Bar Gallery, Dublin *
      Galleri S.E., Bergen
      'In Visible Light', Moderna Museet, Stockholm *
      'Wrapped', West Scaland Museum of Art, Soro *
      'Ceaseless', Crown Center Gallery, Chicago
      'This Island Earth', An Tuireann, Portree *
      'Arena', Kunsthalle im Rathaus, Munich *
      'Host', Tramway, Glasgow
      'Receptor', Galerie H.S. Steinek, Vienna
      'Kick Off', Musée Geo Charles, Echiroles
      Lotta Hammer Gallery, London
      'Nettverk', Museet for Samtidskunst, Oslo *
      'Artcrash', Kulturhus, Arhus
      'Muu Media Festivali', KIASMA, Helsinki *

1997 Johannesburg Biennial *
      'Tales from the City', Stills Gallery, Edinburgh *
      illustrated above: A Short Walk through Sainte Nazaire
      'Verpatchtetes Erbe', Museum fur Kunsthandwerk, Frankfurt
      'Material Culture', Hayward Gallery, London *
      'Materia Europa', Portable Gallery, Amsterdam

Chilling beers in the Bannockburn a month or so after the combined IRA and loyalist ceasefire.

With Leicester-born artist, Jonathan Monk

64

'Ideal Standard Summertime', Lisson Gallery, London

'Karaoke', South London Gallery

'Swarm', SAC Travelling Gallery *
illustrated above left

Eigen + Art at IAS, London

'Sixth International Video Week', Saint-Gervais, Geneva *

1994 'Institute of Cultural Anxiety: Works from the Collection', ICA, London *

'It is not like it used to be', Bartok 32 Galeria, Budapest

'Riviera', Oriel Mostyn, Llandudno * *illustrated above right*

'Fotodiffusion', Turin

'The Curator's Egg', Anthony Reynolds Gallery, London

'Wish you were here', The Bourse, Leeds

'Modern Art', Transmission Gallery, Glasgow

'Gol!', Mark Boote Gallery, New York

'Scottish Video', Museum of Installation, London

1993 'Left Luggage', Paris

'Wonderful Life', Lisson Gallery, London

'Coalition', CCA, Glasgow

'International Departures', Die Gesellschaft für Aktuelle Kunst, Bremen *

selected press

Susanna Beaumont, 'The future's bright', *Scotland on Sunday Magazine*, September 2000

Moira Jeffrey, 'Beer Faced Cheek', *Sunday Herald Directory*, September 2000

Ephraim Webber, 'Take me out of the ball park', *Graphotism*, Issue 20, May 2000

Martin Vincent, 'Arts New Top Ten', *News North West*, May 2000

Robert Dawson Scott, 'Prize win puts video artist on fast forward', *The Scotsman*, April 2000

Phil Miller, 'Scottish artist takes breath away with video of "Urban game"', *The Scotsman*, April 2000

Charles Darwent, 'A new spirit is stirring in young British artists', *The Independent on Sunday*, March 2000

Rachel Campbell-Johnston, 'And it's Beck's with a top No.1 crop', *The Times*, March 2000

Ann Donald, 'Fresh breath is given an airing', *The Herald*, March 2000

Waldemar Januszczak, 'The Futures look bright', *The Sunday Times*, Culture Section, March 2000

Dominique Paini, 'Le Retour du flâneur', *Art Press*, Issue 225, March 2000

Elisabeth Mahoney, 'Buchanan gets ready to play video games on Dundee', *The Scotsman*, February 2000

Jean-Marc Huitorel, 'L'effet traveling. Another Country', *Art Press*, Issue 253, January 2000

Mathieu Marguerin interview, 'Global Game', *Blocnotes*, Number 17, Autumn 1999

Artist's pages, *Blocnotes*, Number 17, Autumn 1999

Patricia Ellis, 'Smells Like Teen Spirit', *Flash Art*, October 1999

Pascal Beausse, 'Nouveaux scenarios sportifs', *Le Journal* (Centre National de la Photographie), September 1999

Celia Loubet interview, 'Le regard des vidéastes sur l'an 2000', *Le Dauphine Liberé*, September 1999

Richard Dorment, 'All the fun of the Art Fair', *The Daily Telegraph*, June 1999

Pal Boyesen interview, *KIT magazine*, Number 17, December 1998

Evelyne Jouanno, 'Roderick Buchanan', *Flash Art*, Number 203, November/ December 1998

Michael Ellis, 'This Island Earth', *Art Monthly*, Issue 219, September 1998

Daniel Jewesbury, *Circa Magazine*, Issue 84, 1998

68   Jean Marc Huitorel, 'Le Terrain des Sports', *Art Press*, Issue 237, July/August 1998

Padraig Timoney, 'Play / Record', *Frieze*, Issue 40, May 1998

John Beagles, 'Tales from the City', *The List*, Issue 316, October 1997

Charles Esche, 'Collision Discourse', *Coil Magazine*, Issue 5, October 1997

Susanna Beaumont, 'Club Land', *The List*, Issue 316, September 1997

Gilda Williams, 'A League of His Own', *Art Monthly*, Issue 209, September 1997

Martin Herbert, 'Roderick Buchanan', *Time Out*, June 1997

Artist's book, 'Yankees', *Art Metropole*, Toronto, February 1997

David Perreau interview, 'Roderick Buchanan', *Documents sur l'Art*, Issue 10, Winter 1996

Robert Garnett, 'A frame of two halfs', *Tate Magazine*, Summer 1996

Lynn MacRitchie, 'Buchanan: Man of the Match', *Financial Times*, June 1996

Krudy Tamas, 'A Kocsma az en Muzeumom', *Magyar Narancs*, November 1995

Judith Findlay, 'Roderick Buchanan "Work in Progress"', *Flash Art*, January 1995

Szoboszlai Janos, 'Csac R & R, De Nekem Tetszik', *Balkon Magazine*, July 1994

Neil Trotter, 'Viva Townhead', *The Big Issue*, No. 28, July 1994

Ross Sinclair, 'Global Village Idiots', *Frieze*, Issue 16, May 1994

Artist's pages, *Portfolio Magazine*, Issue 20, 1994

Artist's pages, *Creative Camera*, Issue 315, May 1992
illustrated above left

Artist's pages, cover and centre spread, *Variant*, Autumn 1988,

Artist's Acknowledgements

Roderick Buchanan would like to thank Jackie, Archie, the Buchanan family and the Donachie family, Galerie Praz-Delavallade, and those who co-operated on the following works:

Ten in a Million: Nantes, Etienne Oudart; Glasgow, Dave Allen; Budapest, Beáta Veszely; Manchester, Tim Wilcox; Berlin, Dave Allen; New York, Warren Neidich; Vienna, Julien Robson; Trondheim, Jeremy Welsh; Amsterdam, Ross Sinclair
Editors: Duncan Finnigan, Peter McCaughey, Paul Cameron, Mike Kelly, Holger Mohaupt

Chasing 1,000: Paul Maguire

Gobstopper: Jim & Stella Buchanan, Alan, Alasdair & Daniel Dimmick, Matthew McGill, Megan Morrison, Jim Rusk, Jonathon and Hannah Terrel

Out: Shaun McBeath, Roland Denning, Derrick Peters, Lucien Grieve, Cameron Mercer, Colin Ruscoe, Carol Salter, Mike Stubbs, Chris Osborne, Katrina Brown, Colour Film Services, Robin Nesbitt at The Factory

Peloton: Ami Barak, FRAC Languedoc Roussillon

Sodastream: Chris Evans, Shona McMullan, Iain Kettles, Richard Wright Charles Esche

Endless Column: Jacqueline Donachie

Change Up: Peter McCaughey, Lagoon Leisure Centre, Duncan Finnigan

Turnaround: Susan May, Belinda Guidi, Holger Mohaupt, Douglas and David Gordon, Mario Codognato, Christine Borland

Deadweight: Susie Hunter, Timorous Beasties Ali McAuley and Paul Simmons

Players: Columbia University, Karun Singh

Work in Progress: All the regular five-a-side players at Townhead

Coast to Coast, Dennistoun: All those that hang out on Duke Street and the Parade

DCA Exhibition: Russell Henderson at 55°, GMACK, GHS Scotland, Tom Cullen and MNS Photocolour

Published to coincide with the
exhibition *Roderick Buchanan 'Players'*
at Dundee Contemporary Arts
25 November 2000 – 4 February 2001
With support from the Hope Scott Trust

ISBN 0 9535178 4 5

Edition of 1,500
© Roderick Buchanan, Dundee Contemporary Arts and the authors
Photography by Roderick Buchanan, Alan Dimmick,
Colin Ruscoe and Simon Starling
Designed by Dalrymple
Printed by BAS

Dundee Contemporary Arts
152 Nethergate · Dundee DD1 4DY

Director: Andrew Nairne
Curator: Katrina Brown
Gallery Manager: Chris Osborne
Assistant Curator: Rob Tufnell

T +44 (0)1382 606220
F +44 (0)1382 606221
E dca@dundeecity.gov.uk
www.dca.org.uk

NEWLAND

Exhibition equipment sponsored
and supplied by Newland Electronics Limited

Dundee Contemporary Arts
is supported by